# .pole story

## ESSAYS ON THE POWER OF EROTIC DANCE

### CLAIRE GRIFFIN STERRETT

**PHOTOGRAPHS BY** GEORGE GRIGORIAN

**EDITED BY** DR. CINDY SHEARER

**COVER & BOOK DESIGN BY** MADE BY M.

**GRIFFIN STERRETT, CLAIRE**
**POLE STORY: ESSAYS ON THE POWER OF EROTIC DANCE**
ISBN-13: 978-0615475042 (THE POLE STORY)

ISBN-10: 0615475043

# Acknowledgements

*Thank you to my family for trusting in me, believing in me and supporting me, even if you don't always agree with me! I love you. Thank you to Jack Gaffney and Trisha Stone of Bad Kitty Exoticwear for being such huge supporters of The Pole Story and the pole dance industry.*

*Thank you to all my friends who read my blog, give me feedback and love and especially to my friends who dance with me. I love you ladies and I could not do this without you by my side.*

*And of course, thank you to Tara Moore, for getting me started on this journey, and to Sheila Kelley, Janelle Giumarra and S Factor studios for walking the path with me.*

*Special Thanks To Brad for his unwavering faith in me and for pushing me to pursue my dreams.*

66 *The erotic is something we've been forbidden for so long we can only define what it means by crawling out from the oppression that we've had surrounding all of our sexuality. It's really important that we recover that power, and I sometimes think that it is only the bravest women who will fight hard enough to recover that.* 99

Nikki Roberts, from *Stripping In Time*

# Préface

The room is dark, so dark that it takes almost a half minute for your eyes to adjust. When they do, the first thing you notice is the reddish glow cast from a single lamp in the corner of the room. Next, you see three silver poles, each about ten feet in height from the floor to the ceiling, placed throughout the room. The room has wood floors, and along one side five women lounge on a bench covered in silk pillows. In the far corner of the room, another woman sprawls in a giant, overstuffed armchair. Her head drops back, her arms rest lightly on the pillows and her legs relax open.

Music starts. It is deafeningly loud. Somewhere in the middle of the room, a female shape stretched out on the floor begins to move slowly. The women on the bench erupt into cheers. The woman on the floor moves her hips and butt in an impossibly slow circle-her long blonde hair cascades down her back and her eyes peer seductively at the women from underneath the rim of the baseball hat she wears. Her body is thick and voluptuous. As she arches her head back, the baseball cap tumbles off her head and onto the floor. She continues to dance, reaching out for the hat, putting it on and letting it fall off again, and you get the sense that she has a connection to this object, that it means something to her.

She is not performing; she is telling the audience an emotionally charged story. Wrapping one hand around the pole, she swings a leg out, her body lifts graciously into the air, and she twirls back down to the floor again this time on all fours. She looks aroused, angry, sad, in love and elated all at the same time. Her movement allows moments of release from pent-up energy. Sometimes she demands your attention, sometimes she asks for it, and other times she simply offers herself to you. At one point, she peels off her tank top and the women cheer even louder. She crawls, slinky and slow and cat-like in the direction of the armchair.She brushes lazily against the woman's body, pressing her body close and circling her hips. The woman in the armchair simply lays back and receives the movements. The dance is both deliberate and careless. She does what feels good to her, not what looks good to you. She expresses her inner emotional state, her desires, her rage, and her fears. She is empowered.

# Contents

# introduction

66 *It's not simply that so many of us are uncomfortable about sexuality.* **It's the relationship that individuals and the culture have with that discomfort**. *The discomfort does not get discussed honestly, nor do most people feel in any way obligated to resolve these feelings. Instead, the discomfort is considered normal and fixed, and the objects of discomfort – sexual words, music, art, and expression-are the things considered expendable.* 99

Marty Klein, PhD.

The dance I described is happening in pole dance studios across the country. While it may sound like what happens in strip clubs, there are several key differences. First, there are no men in the classes. In fact, in most studios, there are no men allowed in the studio. Period. This difference means that in pole dance studios women focus on discovering their own desires and fantasies rather than trying to fulfill men's. This type of discovery can unfold more comfortably in an environment where women do not feel pressured to be desirable for someone else and do not feel endangered for putting their sexuality on full display. Women of all different shapes, ages and sizes participate in pole dance classes. Amazingly enough, as these women learn to move in a sensual way that feels good to them, they look and feel more beautiful. Women who pole dance become more confident and comfortable with their sexuality.

Despite these benefits, pole dancing remains stigmatized, and a woman's decision to pole dance tends to raise eyebrows…and questions. For example, how does vulnerability or embodying the feminine in the interest of exploring sexuality benefit women? Is taking pleasure in being looked at, or being the object of a gaze, perverse or empowering? How and why should we give women space to explore their subjective experience of sexual desire? Our culture gives women mixed messages about their sexuality and pole dancing can be a healthy way for them to work through these messages individually.

On the one hand women are given a great deal of visual imagery from the media on how they should dress and behave - usually for someone else. Television, print, and the Internet all tell women what constitutes a sexy woman and what their bodies should look like. Women learn that sexiness is about looking good and subscribing to a very narrow cultural definition of *beautiful*: thin, long-legged, and busty. However, if they take this direction to the extreme, our culture also perceives them as weak and as subservient to a patriarchal value system. They also risk judgment from other women. For example, a woman who dresses provocatively and alters her appearance physically in order to be considered more attractive risks being labeled a "slut" by her peers. However, if women ignore these media messages entirely, they are perceived as being too masculine and lacking in feminine attributes. One needs to look no further than Hillary Clinton, who is often criticized for being too much of a "man" to see that a lack of sensuality is considered a strike against a woman. I work hard to own my sexuality and believe it is mine to share (or not share) with whomever I please. Women like me are often considered loose or whores. My lack of modesty, and the pleasure I take in being a sensual woman, gets misinterpreted as a lack of self-respect or worse yet, a lack of respect for others. Americans have given women very little space to explore and unleash their sexuality without fear of being judged. And this is quite deliberate. Female sexuality is the seat of every woman's power. It is wrapped up in her ability to create, to give birth, and to give life. And it resides in her body.

If you aren't sure about how this applies to you or what your beliefs about sexuality are, then I hope you'll keep reading. The following essays explore pole dancing and female sexuality, and how these two topics mesh together, overlap and serve one another. They also shed light on why the pole dancing movement has grown in popularity and the ways in which pole dancing can be deeply beneficial to women physically and emotionally - through discovering pleasure in being the object of someone's gaze, or through the joy of feeling alive in one's own body. With that said, I would like to make it clear that how a woman chooses to relate to her sexuality is personal, and I by no means think that my choices, or the choices of pole dancers are for everyone. I understand that to many people, what I am doing and what the pole and exotic dance community are doing seems dangerous, because we are promoting a vision of women that is provocative and therefore hazardous. The assumption, then, must be that I'm misguided. However, I would ask that in the spirit of friendship and true solidarity, you become curious about your own reactions to my choices and let that curiosity lead you to learning more about what you want for yourself.

My experience as a pole dancer has taught me that women make well-informed and judicious decisions about their sexuality when they have an experience of and relationship to the feeling of desire that resides in their body, rather than just an intellectual relationship with it. One of the most effective ways to explore sexual desire (which is a bodily experience) is through movement or dance, particularly erotic movement. If a young woman, through erotic dance in an all-female studio, can begin to feel in her body what she likes and doesn't like, what feels good to her and what doesn't, if she can begin to relate to her sexuality, not just as being accessible to a man, but as something that is hers - to share or not share - then perhaps she will carry that out into the world, into her interactions with men and women. And if she does, then she will be better equipped to know, through her own internal direction and guidance, what she wants and doesn't want when it comes to sex. And, to come full circle, this is a very INDIVIDUAL decision. Perhaps she enjoys being watched, perhaps she doesn't. Perhaps she wants to push hard against her lover, and perhaps she wants him to submit, or push back. And perhaps all of this changes from moment to moment.

For example, I've learned that being

4

vulnerable in front of others in my dancing and being the object of another's gaze in my dance class can be incredibly empowering. My dance classes, however, are all female, there are no mirrors, and I get nothing but love and support reflected back at me. I have danced in public only once, and while it was initially intimidating and there were moments of hesitation, I felt totally empowered by the experience, thrilled to share my dance, my eroticism, and my sexuality with others. I was pleased that it was actually well received and appreciated by men and women alike. There was one moment in the beginning of my dance where I was swinging slowly around the pole in my hoodie, and a woman yelled at me to "Take it off". For a second I was confused and unsure how to respond. Was she being disrespectful? Was I being objectified? I let my body take over and I ended up looking straight at her and smiling. "Do you want me to take it off?" I purred. She was grinning and nodded enthusiastically. I smiled and pulled off my sweatshirt, slowly, enjoying the tease. Was she eager to see me in a tank top? Maybe. Was she trying to embarrass or degrade me? Probably not. Was she projecting her own desire to peel away layers, to play with her sexuality? Possibly. One thing that became very clear to me after performing in public was this: every person in the audience is projecting their sexual fantasy or frustration, their belief systems and their hang-ups about sex onto you. And because you are putting your sexuality on display, they not only feel entitled to do so, they are also pretty sure that whatever they are projecting onto you is not a projection at all, but rather who and what you are.

All that being said, there is still something deeply fulfilling to me about embodying the female erotic and sharing it with others through dance. When I dance, I feel like I am conquering my fears of being seen and judged. I feel like I'm offering my audience a delicious gift. And I feel a great sense of physical and athletic accomplishment as well. It's my hope, that through dialogue and education, we can begin to see the value in pole dance and the value in the exploration of it, even if we choose not to share it with anyone or to explore the movement ourselves.

Each of these essays began as blogs on my website, *www.polestory.com*. They range from topics like pole dancing as an Olympic sport to the psychological and emotional benefits of pole. I invite you to stay in a conversation with me about the book and what you may have learned through my site, and I welcome and look forward to your comments.

# POLE DANCING IS EMPOWERING

**E**mpowerment: a word many women use to describe their experience of pole dancing. It's also a word that other people tend to get a bit twitchy about when it gets used in conjunction with pole dancing. How can something that has been so strongly associated with the objectification and demoralization of women be called empowering? What on earth could be empowering about dancing in only a bikini and six inch stilettos? The answers to these questions lie in understanding why some don't see pole dancing as empowering and why they feel the need to marginalize those who pole dance.

Because pole dancers are linked (and to some extent rightfully so) with the strip club community and because we live in a culture where overt displays of female sexuality are seen as "less than desirable", it's not surprising that many dancers feel judged for their decision to dance, and that there is objection and prejudice from the general public when it comes to pole dancing. When people outside the community ridicule the idea of a pole dancing class as empowering, or another woman accuses pole dancers of "betraying women everywhere", and none of these people have ever even set foot inside of a studio, it seems like what dancers are experiencing is an attempt at exclusion from the wider circle of society. That exclusion is frequently based on fear and misunderstanding. Interestingly enough, many people are basing their grounds for objection on the fact that pole dancing is "denigrating" to women. They want to judge and subsequently ostracize something that they have never experienced, know nothing about and have never bothered to research. They often make judgments in the spirit of protecting women and their integrity. These judgments feel hypocritical to women, like me, who are pole dancers since we feel we are protecting and taking care of ourselves by inquiring into our sexuality as well as giving ourselves rigorous physical training. Also, our views are based on experience, not just on an idea of what pole dancing is.

David Mitchell in an article for *The Guardian* that ran in April 2010, criticized The University of Cambridge's decision to offer all-female pole dance classes. He suggested that University-sponsored pole dance classes are a large step in the *wrong* direction for women. But Mitchell relies on misconceptions about the pole dance community as well as a few deeply ingrained myths and biases toward women and sexuality to make his point. For example, he refers to a woman who might be interested in a pole dancing class as "stupid and impressionable". He suggests that the only reason women might be taking these classes is in order to be "ogled" by men. He also argues that the dance classes are sexist, because they exclude men.

In keeping with the views of society, Mitchell tries to marginalize women in the pole dancing community. And this is not uncommon. Pole dancing is an activity that pushes boundaries, especially when it comes to female sexuality. Ten years ago you would have been hard-pressed to find a pole dancing class in most U.S. cities. Gaining mainstream acceptance has only just begun. Now you can find pole dance classes in major gyms across the country and it is rapidly becoming a respected form of fitness. There is a growing community of women who freely choose to dance sensually on a pole in six-inch stilettos, however, it is *not* the social norm. And for men, it is even less so.

Yet most women who have taken a pole dancing class for any extended period of time will say that they have increased their confidence – physically and oftentimes sexually as well. They will often use the word "empowered" to describe their experiences in pole dance classes. Empowerment refers to increasing the spiritual, political, social or economic strength of individuals and communities. It involves individuals developing confidence in their personal capacities. So how does pole dancing fit into that definition?

*Economically*, women in the pole dancing community are starting their own businesses through teaching, writing, clothing sales, competitions and making money, developing a new niche market, and spending their own money for something they see as valuable.

*Politically*, women in the pole dancing community are pushing to redefine the limits of what is seen as appropriate sexual behavior for women, pushing to be seen as athletes in their own right, pushing for the freedom to express sexuality and sensuality without marginalization or condemnation.

*Socially*, women in the pole dancing community are gathering and connecting, building relationships, networking, supporting one another, getting fit, exploring their femininity, embracing their sexuality, playing, laughing, crying and celebrating one another.

*Spiritually*, women in the pole dancing community are connecting to "the erotic", which is a deeply feminine and deeply spiritual place in everyone. The erotic is linked to an internal knowing, a felt sense that lives in the body. Additionally, women in the pole dancing community are gathering in the same way that many spiritually-based organizations gather: once a week, in a designated sacred space, with the intention of communing individually and collectively in honor of their bodies and their movement.

When we look at pole dancing from this perspective, it makes the idea that women are taking pole dance classes simply to be "ogled" seem absurd. First of all, the reason pole dancing classes are all female is specifically to avoid the "ogling" factor, and not because they are sexist, as Mr. Mitchell would have us believe. Secondly, so *what* if a woman enjoys the gaze of another person while dancing erotically. What is *wrong* with that? I'll tell you why our culture thinks it's wrong. Anyone who has ever danced erotically for another knows the tremendous power she has over that person. The quickest way to rob a woman of that power is to shame her out of it. And that's the dirty little trick that's been played on women for centuries. Unfortunately, we play into it by allowing and sometimes even encouraging demeaning responses to our sexuality. It's only by fully owning and expressing our sexual selves that we will put an end to that nasty practice. Pole dancing, as most of us know already, is an excellent way of doing just that.

# TAKE IT

**I**'m always slightly amused by pole dancing studios that insist on stating that there
is NO STRIPPING involved in their classes.
As if somehow this assertion will insure that no
one will confuse what happens in their studio
with what happens in strip clubs. As if what distinguishes stripping and pole dance classes is the
removal of clothing.

I actually strip in my dance classes. I strip
down to a thong and a bra. Not every class,
and when I do strip, not every layer always
comes off. But I take my clothes off. You see, I
think the act of stripping off layers is important
for a couple of reasons. First, it's an art form.
Getting out of your clothes gracefully while
dancing, mastering the art of the tease takes
tremendous talent and practice.

According to Lucinda Jarrett, author of
*Stripping in Time*, stripping is actually a unique-
ly American art form. It was here in the U.S. that
the art of striptease was first recognized as a
craft. Back in the twenties, strippers dubbed

themselves "ecdysiasts" and schools for teaching the art of walking, posing and peeling sprung up everywhere. Once these parts were mastered, and the women gained sufficient confidence, they would bring their own personalities into the act, including costumes. How much one could reveal without revealing it all was the name of the game. In our current culture, where baring it all seems to have become the norm (think of *Girls Gone Wild* videos where women display their breasts for a half second in exchange for beads, or photos of various panty-less starlets exiting vehicles), there is something to be said for the sensual art of revealing one's self slowly and deliberately.

Secondly, there is an emotional component to stripping that is extraordinarily enticing to me. There is something so freeing about shedding your clothing, layer by layer. I love pulling at the hem of my shirt while I swing around the pole or feeling my ankles get tangled up in a miniskirt that has found its way down my legs. I take real pleasure in revealing myself to my classmates, layer by layer. That pleasure comes from the understanding that my vulnerability and my power are inextricably mixed up in this process. In revealing myself, I make myself vulnerable. But the act of revealing myself also holds my audience captive and mesmerized, which feels powerful.

A few years ago I saw a play called *The Why Factor*. In this play, a group of women decide to take pole dancing classes for various personal reasons, which are revealed to the audience as the play progresses. There was one scene in particular that struck an emotional chord with me, and it had to do with stripping. One day in class the women are challenged by their teacher to "peel off their layers". This metaphor for taking off one's clothes is in this case symbolic of taking off the layers of bandages that we put over our emotional wounds. During the following monologue, Pele, who is the teacher, begins to take her own layers off:

> 66 *Now we're getting somewhere. Peel it off Verne. Peel off the layers. Maybe then you will be able to figure out why you said yes. Maybe then you will be able to feel something.* 99

> *(PELE has begun to circle the room, continuing to peel layers off her clothing. The goddess is beginning to get angry)*

> 66 *Would that be so bad? Would opening your legs lead to opening your heart? What if it did and what spilled out was dirty, rank sewer water? Could you let that wash over you if it meant ridding yourselves of it once and for all? Or do you want it to stay inside and fester? To pus over and harden, so you can carry it around for everybody to share? Is that what all of you want?* 99

> *(she strips off more clothing)*

> 66 *Is that what you're afraid of? Your truth?* 99

The monologue reflects some of what I find so powerful about the process of peeling away clothing from our bodies: it's about revealing our sexuality deliberately and slowly, about exposing our most vulnerable selves. There can be something very emotionally potent about the act of stripping. As Catherine Roach says so eloquently in her book *Stripping, Sex and Popular Culture*, stripping can become a metaphor for taking off inhibitions, such as shame, guilt, fear and ignorance. It can become a way of *stripping* off narrow definitions of beauty and sexiness, and the oppression of those who enjoy sexual pleasure outside of the norm.

There is a common misperception that stripping is about exposure and overexposure. I disagree. When I remove my clothes, I am choosing to *reveal* parts or even all of my body to another. I am stripping away my inhibitions and shame over my body. I'm defying the demand that society makes of me to keep it under wraps, to cover it up, to restrict my appetite. I am reveling in the pleasure of offering something delicious to another. I am enjoying the playfulness of teasing my audience.

So the next time you are swinging around that pole or rolling around on the floor, put on an extra layer or two first, and slowly, sensually, deliberately *take it off*!

# silent bodies

WHY POLE DANCING MIGHT BE ESSENTIAL
FOR SOME YOUNG WOMEN

I dance at S Factor studios. In the S factor curriculum, instructors ask students to focus on how they feel in their bodies when they are dancing. They spend a lot of time on floor work, which gets students out of their heads. They encourage students to slow down and pay attention to their breath. But most of all, they encourage their students to pay attention to what they are feeling in their bodies as they move. I feel a lot of different things in my body when I dance--anger, shame, fear, joy, sadness, exhaustion. But my own desire is a part of every movement I make. I move my body in a way that feels right to me. I've learned to touch myself and experience the sensual pleasure of running my hand across my breasts or belly. In doing so, I have not only awakened sexual desire in my body, I've learned what my body wants and what this wanting feels like. Pole dancing, such as the kind I do at S Factor, occurs in a safe, all-female environment—and encourages women to get to know their desires and bodies.

But a healthy exploration of sexuality and desire can get mistaken for an unhealthy obsession with sex and exposure. In her book *Female Chauvinist Pigs*, Ariel Levy takes a chapter to talk about how "Raunch Culture" is affecting young women. "Raunch Culture" , as defined by Levy, is the pornification of femininity and is demonstrated through things like unhealthy and unattainable role models of female beauty and a willingness to engage in casual sexual behavior. Levy points out that female adolescents, who are already dealing with raging hormones, peer pressure, and the need to fit in, are being bombarded with images of sexiness in the media and being pressured to look sexy while simultaneously being told through abstinence-only programs not to have sex. She argues that we are doing very little to help girls distinguish their sexual desires from their desires for attention. The sad thing about this, she says, is that from the beginning of their experiences as sexual beings, they regard sex as a performance that you give for attention, rather than something thrilling that you engage in because you want to. On all these points, I could not agree more with Levy. But here is where we disagree: she includes the rampant popularity of pole dancing classes in her definition of "Raunch Culture." Levy demonstrates a very limited understanding of what happens in a pole dancing class, as well as ignorance about how it can be a potential solution to the problem she describes in teenagers.

Levy refers to Deborah Tolman, a psychologist who has researched and written extensively on teen girls and sexuality, to support her argument against "Raunch Culture," pole dancing included. Tolman talks to girls about their experience of "wanting" versus their experience of "sex", which is more often than not about being wanted. Tolman (and Levy) use the phrase "silent bodies" to describe the sexual experiences of these young girls. Whether or not these young women had sex, they had a difficult time expressing if or how they felt desire or arousal in their bodies. They instead chose to muffle their feelings, out of fear for where it might take them, out of shame and out of anxiety. Nevertheless, they were still engaging in sexual activities and, more often than not, these activities were described as having "just happened" to them. Tolman points out that not feeling any sexual desire can put young women at great risk. "When a girl does not know what her own feelings are, when she disconnects the apprehending psychic part of herself from what is happening in her own body, she then becomes especially vulnerable to the power of others' feelings." Or, as Levy sums it up, you have to know what you want in order to know what you don't want. Levy is right; however, her conclusions about pole dancing are off and she offers very little in terms of solutions.

In her book *Dilemmas of Desire*, Tolman argues that sexual desire, in and of itself, is not dangerous, essentially masculine, or monstrous. It's a part of our relational world, a sign of our connection to our own bodies, and our connection to other people. Basing her argument on Jean Baker Miller's assertion that sexual authenticity (the ability to bring one's own real feelings of sexual desire and sexual pleasure meaningfully into intimate relationships) is a key feature of women's psychological health, Tolman says that the body is the counterpart of the psyche engaged in the ongoing process of constructing a subjective sense of one's sexuality. "Desire is a form of knowledge, gained through the body: In desiring, I know I exist."

If what these authors are saying is true, then teaching young women how to develop a subjective sense of their sexual selves would actually be a solution to them giving away their sexuality. In other words, our culture needs to teach women how to get in touch with what desire and arousal feels like, how to experience it in their bodies, and how to express what they want and don't want. Pole dancing is an excellent vehicle for such an education. When Ariel Levy talks about the pornification of our culture, I think what she is talking about is the extent to which she sees women, young and not-so-young, imitating or playing at sexiness. There is a difference between a woman who is "acting" sexy for the sake of wanting to be desired by someone or wanting to fit in to something and a woman who is "being" sexy, that is fully embodying her sexuality, and who is fully aware of and owning her desires, without apology and without shame. The former is held captive, and becomes an easy target for other people's desires, because her main objective is to please. The latter is empowered, and will pick and choose with whom she wants to share herself and when, based on her experience of what her body is telling her. But in order to hear her body, she has to learn to listen to it.

The pole dancing experience is exactly what these young women's "silent bodies" are sorely in need of: a way to awaken, to familiarize themselves with and de-stigmatize their experience of desire. If it were up to me, some form of all-girls female erotic dance class would be a part of sex education for women in schools across the country. Women are already bombarded with images of what acting sexy looks like. It's time to teach them what being sexy feels like.

# women
## AND THE GAZE

I did a photo shoot with a very talented artist by the name of Gregory Beylerian. He was interested in capturing some images of women on their poles at home and he was especially interested in capturing the emotions and the sensuality of the dance – much more so than the tricks and technical skills. The experience was sublime. With the exception of my classmates, I rarely dance for others. And when I dance, I let an extremely sensual, extremely erotic part of myself come out to play. This makes me feel equally powerful and vulnerable.

So sharing that part of myself with a near stranger in my living room and subsequently my bedroom was initially nerve-wracking. But as it turns out, I had no trouble at all dropping into that sensual, sexual part of myself in front of another. And after the first couple of songs (and ok fine, one glass of wine) I found that I really enjoyed sharing my sensual self with the camera. I teased and taunted and hid from and seduced the camera with my eyes, my hair, my hips, my back, my breasts and my ass – especially my ass. I told a story with my body, a story of longing for someone to come after me, of wanting to chase and be chased. And while I was doing all of that a funny thing happened: I discovered that I really enjoyed it.

There was something exhilarating and liberating about exposing that part of myself to someone else – someone outside of the studio. More importantly, rather than feeling like an object of the camera's gaze I actually felt like the camera was the object of my gaze. I was in charge. I was the one looking at my audience. I was displaying my sexuality, owning it and forcing it onto the viewers, whomever they might be.

While certainly Gregory put me at ease with his demeanor, I uncovered a part of myself that I did not know existed. At the same time, there were these moments of discomfort where some sort of old programming about what is and isn't appropriate for a woman to be doing with her body would pop into my head (usually when I was pushing things a little bit further – pulling off a layer or rolling around in the bed). In those moments the question "Is this bad?" would rattle around my brain for a few seconds. Literally. And then I would drop my head into a lazy circle, arch my back, circle my hips and think "Well, it feels too good in my body to be bad. So F*@k it." There was nothing passive or powerless about my experience of being photographed.

Feminist critics have always been concerned with how women can transcend objectification. Traditionally, they've associated being the object of a man's gaze with being made into a passive, powerless object of desire. When it comes to sexuality many feminists and women ask: how can women resist being rendered passive by the male gaze? And can they instead, look back at the men?

As a matter of fact, this is exactly what women do in exotic dance. They look back. There is nothing passive about the way in which exotic dancers receive their audience's gaze. Anita Berber, who began performing nude in 1918 in cabarets in Germany, was known for looking back at her audiences. Lucinda Jarrett, author of *Stripping in Time* describes La Goulue, a famous can-can dancer at the Moulin Rouge, as ",.. staring greedily at the crowds, absorbing the desire that shone in their faces, which turned pale under her insolent gaze." These women were not submissive, powerless sexual objects. I didn't feel like a submissive, powerless object in my photo shoot. What distinguishes us from being objectified by the male gaze is our willingness to participate with our audience and, in effect, look back at them: to meet their gaze with our gaze. It takes courage to do this, and there is tremendous power in being able to own one's body and sexuality so forcefully and confidently.

This power, and the pleasure women take in displaying their sexuality is unfortunately precisely what earns them the label "slut" in American culture. We don't like women who dress provocatively or who show off their bodies. We either denigrate them or we pity them as victims of low self-esteem or of abuse. We assume that they take no personal pleasure in their actions. And if they do, then God help them – they need saving. This type of thinking can be seen in the public discomfort caused by female Olympic athletes posing for sexy pictures in Esquire magazine. In general, the display of the female body for athletic purposes is considered respectable. But once the athlete crosses the line into sharing her body in a sensual manner, she has somehow degraded herself, even though the decision to pose in such a manner is her own. In these pictures, the female athletes were striking provocative poses in skimpy clothing or bathing suits. The public responded by accusing the magazine (and, to some extent the athletes) of tarnishing their image as role models.

Feminist concern about the objectification of women is connected to the stigma of the "slut". Women who have openly displayed their appetite for sex or their willingness to engage in sexual behavior have been judged as having loose morals and therefore being "bad". They are bad because they put their sexuality out there and are therefore perceived as encouraging their own (and all women's) objectification. But put in another context, this display could be thought of as a different type of sexual behavior, like homosexuality or bisexuality. Merri Lisa Johnson (former stripper and author of *Consuming and Producing Exotic Dance*) uses the term "stripper sexuality" to describe what she calls a heightened sensuality. Whatever term one uses, this open sexuality often gets pigeonholed as dysfunctional or the unfortunate result of childhood sexual trauma. The common cultural perspective, says Johnson, on stripping or erotic dance is that it takes something away from a woman, whether it is self-respect, self-esteem or freedom. In fact, it could be argued that it is mainstream culture that takes something away – our sexual freedom – and stripping can, in some cases, give it back. Or, stated more precisely, women can take it back. They take it back in the same way they take back the gaze: by challenging the assumptions their audience makes about their willingness to be looked at.

Both the stigma of being objectified and the stigma of being viewed as a slut not only interfere with women's perception of others who are able to transcend these labels, but they also restrict them from enjoying the full spectrum of their sensuality and connecting with their erotic power. And understanding our erotic power, connecting to it, is an essential part of a healthy female psyche.

# Olympics

**M**any women I know in high powered, stressful jobs find that their pole dance classes help them not just to relax, but to feel "like a woman again". Other women who study different forms of sensual dance, such as belly dancing, have echoed this sentiment. In an article in the March 22, 2009 issue of *Washington Post Magazine*, Rachael Galoob was interviewed about her local belly dance studio. Galoob is a former attorney with two law degrees who decided to leave her law career in order to perform and teach. Her students tend to be well-educated professionals in high-powered jobs. Many of them come to belly dance classes in order to reconnect with their feminine side. They claim this sensual movement reduces their stress levels by forcing them to focus on their body and their movement and that it helps them to feel more beautiful. Of course, pole dancing provides women with a very similar outlet. Pole dancing has tremendous value both as an art form and as a tool for healing. It can help women to reconnect with their bodies by providing a space in which they can heal from wounds related to their sexuality. This wounding can be something as simple as needing to learn how to let go of exercising our masculine side and allowing the feminine to come forward. For example, many women have gotten used to behaving in a very masculine way, i.e. directional, goal-oriented, and assertive in order to accomplish certain things in life. There is of course, nothing inherently wrong with this and women have achieved quite a bit in doing so. However, a possible pitfall to over-exercising the masculine is that a woman loses touch with or forgets how to live in the more receptive, more feminine side.

In addition to providing women with a healthy creative outlet, pole dancing is also a beautiful and expressive form of dance. It's filled with graceful aerial tricks, sensual spins, and provocative floor work. Pole dancing evokes a narrative - specific emotions, conflicts and insights. The dancer uses her body to communicate. Pole dancers, through their sensual, fluid movements and the sheer strength involved in some of the moves, evoke arousal and admiration in their audiences. Because many pole dancers are deeply connected to their erotic power, they are able to express their sensuality and femininity through their dance.

Moreover, pole dancing is not about recreating a purity of form in the way that other forms of dance (such as ballet) strive for. While there are certain moves and tricks that can be standardized one of the beautiful things about pole dancing is that it is, as Judith Lynne

Hanna put it "an execution of clear and concise movements and gestures that are expressive of inner states unique to the particular performer, to the passing mood, even to the fleeting instant" (Judith Lynne Hanna). Part of what makes pole dancing so thrilling to watch is the inventiveness and spontaneity of the dancers, and how intensely personal their movements are.

This brings up an important set of questions: If the virtues of pole dancing lay in its spontaneity, its femininity and sensuality, how do we go about mainstreaming it? And is there even any value in making it appealing to the mainstream? Or will it lose its potency?

One way to mainstream pole dancing is through the world of competitive sports. For example, there is an ongoing effort to bring pole dancing to the Olympics. There is concern that if pole dancing does go in this direction, it will lose some of its inherent sensuality. Of course, none of the groups pushing for pole dancing to join the Olympics are saying that this should be the *only* form of pole available to the public. But it does beg the question: what is going to be the primary way in which the general public engages with this art form? Perhaps part of the reason why some dancers oppose having pole dancing in the Olympics is because it would inevitably make that *particular* form of pole dancing (or pole fitness) the most commonly seen and viewed. And many dancers feel that a fitness-based gymnastics form of pole dance is not representative of the art, the soul, or the history of pole dancing.

As dancers, we know in our bodies and in our hearts and souls what this movement does for us. We know subjectively (subjective knowing being a more feminine way of knowing something – based on intuition and a felt body sense) that this movement has touched us, shaped us, woken us up, ignited fires and yes, changed our psyches. In my opinion, the way in which some of the community is seeking to legitimize pole dancing may feel threatening not just because it approaches the movement in a way that feels restrictive, but because it is basically saying to those of us that already know what we feel in our bodies, "Well, that's not good enough." Not only would the more feminine, empowering parts of this dance be at risk of being lost, but we would feel told that the very experience each of us has in our bodies is not a "legitimate" source of information. I think that would be deeply hurtful to the feminine – whose primary power and source of knowledge is the sensate, the body. And it is a larger symptom of our culture's dismissal and critique of the body as a source of knowledge.

Trying to turn pole dancing into an Olympic sport if you are in it for the art form, the sensual aspects, the engagement with that deeply feminine part of yourself, is in some ways, taking a very feminine experience and forcing it into the more masculine, objective world of measurements, restrictions, linear direction and goals. When we do this, we risk losing the flavor, the power, and the feminine essence of the movement. This concerns me not because I think that pole dancing would become vertical gymnastics, but because vertical gymnastics would become the standard of pole dancing. In other words, competitors will be judged on the flawlessness of their tricks on the pole much like gymnastic competitors are judged on the flawlessness of their tricks on the balance beam. Instead of allowing a woman's natural sensuality and sexiness to unfold on stage, we would ask her to present a sanitized version of what was once a deeply sexual movement. Instead of asking our country to look at it's own deeply imbedded cultural biases and fears around female sexuality, we would give them something that makes them feel comfortable and allows those prejudices to go unexamined.

As pole dancers, we have a very real opportunity to shift the way the public views female sexuality. It's not going to be easy, and there is no guarantee of success, but in my opinion, it's deeply important for women everywhere. In that regard, this push for the Olympics has done something positive by thrusting pole dancing into the public spotlight. Erotic dance is an excellent mirror for our culture's sex phobia, and the Olympic debate is forcing people's prejudices, fears and beliefs into plain view. This is good because it allows these beliefs to be examined, instead of festering in the unspoken unconscious somewhere. So, in some ways, this change has already begun. But much remains ahead of us. It is my personal hope that, no matter where we end up, pole dancing retains its erotic, sensual, striptease roots.

# WOMEN & THEIR EROTIC
# power

Sexuality is primarily experienced in the body. While there are a number of ways to explore sexual repression in women, few of them address the body. When one is able to be "embodied" (present in their body both emotionally and physically) the exploration of sexuality can be significantly deepened and many of the underlying psychological issues related to sexuality and the body can be healed.

Dance can be an excellent way to explore sexuality and embodiment, particularly erotic dance. The rising popularity of all-female erotic dance classes could be driven by any number of needs: the need to feel something forbidden, to reclaim a lost part of one's self, or simply to feel sexy. Whatever the drive may be, the result is almost always that women are experimenting with reconnecting to a deeply feminine, primal place. And this is the place where erotic power resides.

In her article "Uses of the Erotic", Audra Lorde explains that true erotic power demands that we be in touch with our deepest longing, rather than shying away from it. She believes the erotic acts as a bridge between our conscious mind and our most chaotic, subconscious emotions. Lorde describes this as a type of internal knowing, based on feelings and non-rational knowledge. She asks us to consider the phrase: "It feels right to me". This, she says, is an acknowledgement of the strength of the erotic as a form of true knowledge. Unfortunately, women have come to distrust the power that rises from deep, non-rational knowledge. The erotic has often been misnamed, and is oftentimes used against women. For this reason, women turn away from their erotic power, and as a result it is rarely regarded as a legitimate source of power or information.

In pole dancing, women are encouraged to explore "uses of the erotic" by learning more about what "feels right" to them. While part of the training is athletic, another part is emotional and based on how women express emotion in their bodies. Pole dancers explore what feels good to them in their bodies, and learn to move from a place that is internally guided, or felt.

Another woman who writes about the erotic (but gives it a different name) is a psychologist by the name of Clarissa Pinkola Estes. Estes trained as a Jungian analyst and has studied both clinical psychology and ethnology (ethnology is the study of groups or tribes). She has done extensive research of wolves, and in her book *Women Who Run with Wolves* she draws strong comparisons between women and wolves--their common traits as well as the ways in which they have been misunderstood and persecuted. Estes defines our connection to deep internal knowing or erotic power as "the wild woman". She argues that when women are disconnected from their wild psyche, they suffer. To find themselves, therefore, they must return to "their instinctive lives, their deeper knowing".

In one chapter "The Joyous Flesh", Estes talks about the body as a vehicle for reconnection with a woman's wildish nature. She describes the body as a multilingual being that speaks through color, temperature, subtle movements, and internal sensations such as a leaping heart or a pit in the stomach. She argues that the importance of the body is not its appearance, but its vitality, responsiveness, and endurance. A woman who constantly must monitor her body and its form is robbed of a joyful relationship with it. Estes encourages women to take back their bodies by ignoring popular ideas about what constitutes happiness and oppressive obsessions with body shape. Taking your body back means not waiting or holding back, not restricting your appetite for anything - sex, love, work - just because society tells you that you are too hungry. Rather, women should be living their life full throttle and with tremendous joy. The body, once reclaimed, becomes a tool for gathering information and a source of strength, joy and knowledge for a woman, rather than a source of shame or embarrassment. The purpose of the body (and what constitutes a healthy body) says Estes, is that it *responds*; it can experience a spectrum of feeling, work as it was meant to, and that it is not anesthetized. She beautifully illustrates a connection to a deeper knowledge within a woman that is possible for *every* woman, a knowledge that could also be described as erotic power.

This knowledge, this erotic power, can be deeply threatening to some people. Lorde argues that one reason why the erotic is so feared is because it empowers women; it becomes a lens through which women scrutinize things, which forces women to evaluate what is important to them honestly and in terms of its meaning in their lives, rather than settling for the convenient, the conventional or the safe. She echoes Estes' concerns about living on external guides rather than from internal knowledge and needs. She warns that we should not ignore these erotic guides, lest we conform to certain societal structures that are not based on our needs. She also agrees that when a woman begins to live from the inside out, and is in touch with this deeper knowledge within her, she begins to be responsible for (and is therefore able to reclaim) herself.

Through these teachings, we can begin to understand how connection with the body, with the erotic, the wild woman, gives us deeper knowledge that is deeply nourishing and essential to the healthy psyche of a woman. A woman's authentic connection with her erotic power requires her to be *embodied.* That is, it requires her to feel all the sensations in her body as they arise, along with the inherent emotional notes that accompany these sensations, and it demands that she consciously acknowledge them. Embodiment also requires that we be able to listen to our body's experience and notice the areas that are numb or aching, as well as the areas that are open and filled with pleasure. Sexual embodiment demands that we engage in the sensual pleasures of our bodies, acknowledge the accompanying fear and shame *and then let it all go.*

It seems that one of the most effective ways for women to gain an authentic connection to their sexuality and their erotic power or potential, as Lorde and Estes describe it, is through working directly with, and through the body. Because dance is an avenue for working with the body, and because it is inherently sexual, it is a natural tool for helping women to achieve this connection. Specifically, because erotic dance is overtly sexual, for centuries it has served not just as an entertainment venue for men but as a way for women to express their inherent erotic power to each other, to the gods, and to themselves. Unfortunately, it has also been subverted into a practice that exploits women and encourages shallow representations of femininity and of the act of sex itself.

But what if the movements of erotic dance were removed from the public venue and put in a different environment—an all-female one? How would this change it? This is exactly what is happening across the country with the widespread popularity of all-female exotic dance classes, and the result thus far has been nothing short of a modern-day female awakening.

# SPECIAL THANKS TO THE DANCERS:

### COVER: ESTEE ZAKAR

Miss Trixter 2010 USPDF Champion, Master Instructor

### INTRODUCTION: MINA MORTEZAIE

2010 USPDF Amateur Champion & the 2010 EMW
Bi-Polar Doubles Champion, Instructor Evolve Dance
Studio & Allure Dance Studio

### PAGE 8: JENNIFER CAMAT

Pole Dance Instructor at Allure Dance & Fitness Studio

### PAGE 14 (wishes to remain anonymous)

### PAGE 20: ERIKA LABANSAT

Master Instructor, OC Pole Fitness

### PAGE 26: SWAN WOULARD

Instructor, Xpolesitions

### PAGE 32-33: ESTEE ZAKAR

### PAGE 40: ESTEE ZAKAR

## About the author

Claire Griffin Sterrett was born and raised in Washington, D.C. She moved to Los Angeles in 2000 and started studying pole dancing In 2006 with a woman named Tara Moore. Since then, she has trained at S Factor Studio, Evolve Dance Studio and Rock Angel Dance Studio. She is a PFA certified Pole Dance instructor. In 2008, Claire completed her MA in Somatic Psychology at Santa Barbara Graduate Institute. Her thesis topic? "The Embodiment of Female Sexuality Through Erotic Dance." She was a speaker at the 2010 International Pole Convention in Washington D.C. and the 2011 Pole Dance Convention in West Palm Beach, FL. Claire is passionate about educating the public on the benefits of pole dancing and the ways in which it can help women to reconnect with their sensual, sexual selves. Claire's blog, "The Pole Story", focuses on pole dancing and female sexuality and has been featured on PoleSuperstar.com and PoleSkivvies.com. Claire is also a contributing writer for the Bad Kitty Exotic Wear blog and Vertical Art Fitness Magazine, and her writing has also been published in Pole Spin Magazine, Pole2Pole Magazine and S Factor Magazine.

Made in United States
Cleveland, OH
21 December 2024